COUNTER CULTURE SCRIPTURE & PRAYER GUIDE

COUNTER CULTURE

SCRIPTURE & PRAYER GUIDE

NEW YORK TIMES BESTSELLING AUTHOR

DAVID PLATT

WITH DAVID BURNETTE

TYNDALE
MOMENTUM™

*The nonfiction imprint of
Tyndale House Publishers, Inc.*

Visit Tyndale online at www.tyndale.com.

Visit Tyndale Momentum online at www.tyndalemomentum.com.

TYNDALE, *Tyndale Momentum*, and Tyndale's quill logo are registered trademarks of Tyndale House Publishers, Inc. The Tyndale Momentum logo is a trademark of Tyndale House Publishers, Inc. Tyndale Momentum is the nonfiction imprint of Tyndale House Publishers, Inc., Carol Stream, Illinois.

Counter Culture Scripture and Prayer Guide

Designed by Julie Chen

Published in association with Yates & Yates, LLP (www.yates2.com).

For information about special discounts for bulk purchases, please contact Tyndale House Publishers at csresponse@tyndale.com or call 800-323-9400.

ISBN 978-1-4964-2275-0   Softcover

23 22 21 20 19 18 17
7   6   5   4   3   2   1

CONTENTS

Our God is in the heavens;

he does all that he pleases.

PSALM 115:3

ANGER. DESPAIR. FEAR. WORRY. For Christians who live in a culture like ours, these are all-too-common reactions to an environment that is increasingly hostile to God and his truth. Even basic institutions like marriage are being questioned and undermined. Then, to make things worse, the sheer size and complexity of global problems such as poverty and sex slavery can make us feel helpless. How can we be faithful to Christ in a world like this?

Before we think about engaging culture and standing for Christ, we need to get the right perspective. Yes, the problems we face are serious, but we serve a God who created all things and is sovereign over every detail of his creation. This God has also promised us that his purposes will prevail and that he will never abandon his people. Followers of Christ in all generations have faced opposition and persecution, and God has been faithful to sustain their faith and to empower their witness. "In the world you will have tribulation," Jesus told his disciples. "But take heart; I have overcome the world" (John 16:33). This God-centered focus is the starting point for engaging culture.

LOOKING TO
A SOVEREIGN GOD

ENGAGING CULTURE STARTS with looking to and trusting in
the God who is sovereign over culture. We need his grace,
his wisdom, and his power at work within us if we are to
speak and act in a way that bears witness to the gospel
of Jesus Christ. It is this God-centered and God-exalting
posture that will keep us from despair on the one hand and
self-reliance on the other. As Christians we must be confi-
dent in God.

> We know that for those who love God all things
> work together for good, for those who are called
> according to his purpose.
> ROMANS 8:28

> [God's] dominion is an everlasting dominion, and
> his kingdom endures from generation to generation;
> all the inhabitants of the earth are accounted as

nothing, and he does according to his will among
the host of heaven and among the inhabitants of
the earth; and none can stay his hand or say to him,
"What have you done?"

DANIEL 4:34-35

Now to him who is able to keep you from stumbling
and to present you blameless before the presence of
his glory with great joy, to the only God, our Savior,
through Jesus Christ our Lord, be glory, majesty,
dominion, and authority, before all time and now
and forever. Amen.

JUDE 1:24-25

Responding in Prayer

- Praise God for his sovereignty over all things and
  people. Express your trust in his power and wisdom.
- Pray that God would give you confidence in his
  promises. Ask him to give you faith and hope as you
  seek to follow Christ.
- Pray that your church would depend fully on God
  and the power of the gospel as you speak to various
  issues in your own community.

THE GOSPEL

I am not ashamed of the gospel,

for it is the power of God for salvation

to everyone who believes.

ROMANS 1:16

IF WE BELIEVE that the gospel is truly the lifeblood of Christianity and the foundation for countering culture, then we ought to meditate on it regularly. Christ lived a life of sinless obedience, the life that God requires of us; Christ died on the cross to pay the penalty for our sin; Christ rose from the grave, thereby conquering sin and death; all who repent of their sins and believe in this Christ receive the forgiveness of sins and the free gift of eternal life. That's good news.

The gospel is the foundation for our faith and for our witness to a dark and dying world. We must not leave it behind, as if we can follow Christ in our own strength. And we must not think that the unbelieving world around us will experience real and lasting change through our own courage, compassion, and conviction. No, it's the gospel that saves and transforms people, and it's the gospel that compels us to speak out when we see injustice, to stand up for those who are afflicted, and to hold fast to the truths of God's Word in the face of opposition. This gospel is the very message that unreached peoples from across the globe so desperately need to hear. The gospel is worthy of our continual reflection and worthy of our lives.

HUMBLING OURSELVES BEFORE GOD

THE FIRST STEP in addressing the sins and needs around us is to confess that *we* are sinful and needy. Our role is not to save culture, for "salvation belongs to the LORD" (Jonah 2:9). We need the same Christ that we proclaim to our unbelieving neighbors. Being used by God begins with being forgiven and cleansed by God.

God is "near to the brokenhearted" (Psalm 34:18), and he promises to forgive those who confess their sins (see 1 John 1:9). Followers of Christ ought to confess their sins to God and ask him to strengthen them to be obedient. This kind of humility is pleasing to God and it prepares us to be used by him.

Let anyone who thinks that he stands take heed lest he fall.

I CORINTHIANS 10:12

Have mercy on me, O God, according to your
steadfast love; according to your abundant mercy
blot out my transgressions. Wash me thoroughly
from my iniquity, and cleanse me from my sin!

PSALM 51:1-2

O LORD God of heaven, the great and awesome
God who keeps covenant and steadfast love with
those who love him and keep his commandments,
let your ear be attentive and your eyes open, to
hear the prayer of your servant that I now pray
before you day and night for the people of Israel
your servants, confessing the sins of the people of
Israel, which we have sinned against you. Even I
and my father's house have sinned. We have acted
very corruptly against you and have not kept the
commandments, the statutes, and the rules that
you commanded your servant Moses. Remember
the word that you commanded your servant Moses,
saying, "If you are unfaithful, I will scatter you
among the peoples, but if you return to me and
keep my commandments and do them, though
your outcasts are in the uttermost parts of heaven,
from there I will gather them and bring them to the
place that I have chosen, to make my name dwell
there." They are your servants and your people,
whom you have redeemed by your great power
and by your strong hand. O Lord, let your ear be
attentive to the prayer of your servant, and to the
prayer of your servants who delight to fear your

name, and give success to your servant today, and grant him mercy in the sight of this man.

NEHEMIAH 1:5-11

Responding in Prayer

- Confess your sins to God. Ask him for forgiveness and to grant repentance.
- Pray that God would give you humility as you speak about the gospel and the truths of God's Word. Ask God to remove your own self-righteousness as you confront the sins of others.
- Pray that your church would be known not only for its boldness but also for its humility in your community.

THE FOUNDATION FOR OUR FAITH

CHRIST'S DEATH AND RESURRECTION are the basis for everything the New Testament authors say. Even the Old Testament, Jesus says, was pointing forward to him all along (see Luke 24:44). It's no surprise, then, that Scripture is filled with promises related to the gospel, as well as explanations about the gospel's significance for our lives and our churches. Take time to think through the following passages as you reflect on the glory of the gospel of Jesus Christ.

> The word of the cross is folly to those who are perishing, but to us who are being saved it is the power of God.
>
> I CORINTHIANS 1:18

> I [Paul] delivered to you as of first importance what I also received: that Christ died for our sins in accordance with the Scriptures, that he was buried,

that he was raised on the third day in accordance
with the Scriptures.

I CORINTHIANS 15:3-4

Now the righteousness of God has been manifested
apart from the law, although the Law and the
Prophets bear witness to it—the righteousness of
God through faith in Jesus Christ for all who believe.
For there is no distinction: for all have sinned and
fall short of the glory of God, and are justified by
his grace as a gift, through the redemption that is in
Christ Jesus, whom God put forward as a propitiation
by his blood, to be received by faith. This was to show
God's righteousness, because in his divine forbearance
he had passed over former sins. It was to show his
righteousness at the present time, so that he might be
just and the justifier of the one who has faith in Jesus.

ROMANS 3:21-26

Responding in Prayer

- Thank God for sending his Son to pay the penalty for
  your sins and for raising him from the dead. Ask God
  to help you rely on Christ for your righteousness.
- Ask God to help you trust that the gospel (and
  not your own abilities and efforts) is the power for
  salvation.
- Pray that your church would focus on making
  disciples by proclaiming the gospel of Jesus Christ
  in your community and around the world.

THE GOSPEL AND CULTURE

WHILE THE GOSPEL brings peace between God and sinful men, it also creates conflict—conflict between those who believe the gospel and those who reject it. This kind of conflict should be expected for those who follow Christ (see John 16:33; 2 Timothy 3:12). Speaking and living by the truth is costly. However, the cost of following Christ is as nothing compared to the reward.

In light of the fact that suffering and opposition are expected in the Christian life, it is fitting that God has given us so many promises that assure us of his presence and of our future reward. We would do well to meditate on and memorize these promises, even if we're not presently walking through a trial. Opposition will come, in one form or another, and we should want to be found faithful.

[Jesus] said to all, "If anyone would come after me, let him deny himself and take up his cross daily and follow me. For whoever would save his life will lose it, but whoever loses his life for my sake will save it. For what does it profit a man if he gains the whole world and loses or forfeits himself? For whoever is ashamed of me and of my words, of him will the Son of Man be ashamed when he comes in his glory and the glory of the Father and of the holy angels."

LUKE 9:23-26

Beloved, do not be surprised at the fiery trial when it comes upon you to test you, as though something strange were happening to you. But rejoice insofar as you share Christ's sufferings, that you may also rejoice and be glad when his glory is revealed. If you are insulted for the name of Christ, you are blessed, because the Spirit of glory and of God rests upon you. But let none of you suffer as a murderer or a thief or an evildoer or as a meddler. Yet if anyone suffers as a Christian, let him not be ashamed, but let him glorify God in that name.

I PETER 4:12-16

What then shall we say to these things? If God is for us, who can be against us? He who did not spare his own Son but gave him up for us all, how will he not also with him graciously give us all things? Who shall bring any charge against God's elect? It is God who justifies. Who is to condemn? Christ Jesus is the one who died—more than that, who was raised—who is at the right hand of God, who indeed is interceding for us. Who shall separate us from the love of Christ? Shall tribulation, or distress, or persecution, or famine, or nakedness, or danger, or sword? . . . No, in all these things we are more than conquerors through him who loved us. For I am sure that neither death nor life, nor angels nor rulers, nor things present nor things to come, nor powers, nor height nor depth, nor anything else in all creation, will be able to separate us from the love of God in Christ Jesus our Lord.

ROMANS 8:31-35, 37-39

Responding in Prayer

- Thank God for his promise to be with you and for the hope he has given us in Christ.
- Pray that God would prepare you to faithfully endure trials.
- Ask God to prepare your church for times of opposition. Pray that your pastors and the congregation would hold fast to the gospel.

POVERTY

Whoever closes his ear to the cry of the poor

will himself call out and not be answered.

PROVERBS 21:13

WITH MORE THAN a billion people living in poverty worldwide, the problem can seem so overwhelming that we feel paralyzed and simply block it from our minds. Add to that the allure of money and of pursuing comfort in our culture, and the poor are quickly forgotten. As followers of Christ, however, we do not have the option of ignoring those in need.

God cares for the poor, and he calls his people to do the same. In fact, the way we treat the poor and the way we use our material resources reflect our relationship with God. Hearts transformed by God's mercy will increasingly want to extend that mercy to others. Beginning with our own families, churches, and communities, and then looking out to a world in need, we must ask, *How can I leverage the resources and opportunities God has given me to help meet urgent physical and spiritual needs?* We are not called to solve the problem of poverty ourselves or to feel guilty for what we can't change. However, we should be eager for God to use us and to use our churches for the spread of the gospel and for the good of our neighbors. May God's grace, not guilt, motivate us to care for the poor.

HOW GOD SEES THE POOR

GOD'S CONCERN FOR the poor is evident throughout Scripture. Even when his people were weak and needy, he provided for them and protected them. The world may look down on the poor, but God often demonstrates his mercy and grace toward those who are least esteemed in the world's eyes.

> [God] delivers the needy when he calls, the poor and him who has no helper. He has pity on the weak and the needy, and saves the lives of the needy.
>
> PSALM 72:12-13

> [The Lord] has brought down the mighty from their thrones and exalted those of humble estate; he has filled the hungry with good things, and the rich he has sent away empty.
>
> LUKE 1:52-53

Listen, my beloved brothers, has not God chosen
those who are poor in the world to be rich in faith
and heirs of the kingdom, which he has promised to
those who love him?

JAMES 2:5

Responding in Prayer

- Thank God for his compassion for the weak and
  needy.
- Ask God to help you show mercy toward the poor
  around you. As you look for ways to minister, pray
  that God would make you aware of needs around you.
- Pray that God would guard you from preferring those
  with money and influence in your community.

HOW WE SHOULD
TREAT THE POOR

OUR RESPONSE TO the poor should reflect God's own concern for them. He has commanded us to care for those in need and to give justice to those who are afflicted. Rather than pursuing wealth and selfishly living for our own comfort, we are to give generously in light of how much God has given us. In short, we are to love all of our neighbors as ourselves.

> If among you, one of your brothers should become poor, in any of your towns within your land that the LORD your God is giving you, you shall not harden your heart or shut your hand against your poor brother.
>
> DEUTERONOMY 15:7

> If anyone has the world's goods and sees his brother in need, yet closes his heart against him, how does God's love abide in him?
>
> I JOHN 3:17

Give justice to the weak and the fatherless; maintain
the right of the afflicted and the destitute. Rescue
the weak and the needy; deliver them from the hand
of the wicked.

PSALM 82:3-4

Responding in Prayer

- Ask God to strengthen your faith so that you might
  gladly share your resources with those in need.
- Pray for the courage to speak up on behalf of the poor.
- Pray that God would use your church to minister to
  the physical and spiritual needs of the poor in your
  community.

ABORTION

You formed my inward parts;

you knitted me together

in my mother's womb.

PSALM 139:13

OVER FORTY-TWO MILLION abortions occur worldwide every year.[1] That's 115,000 individuals created in the image of God who are killed every single day. It's no wonder that, for Christians, this issue brings up feelings of sadness, anger, and, given the size of the problem, helplessness. We must depend on God as we respond to abortion.

Scripture tells us that God has a special relationship with the unborn, for he has created these precious children, and he knows them intimately. It's only natural, then, that God's people would be concerned for the well-being of the unborn. We must speak up for those who have no voice and work for their protection. At the same time, we must minister to mothers considering abortion and point them to the hope that can only be found in Christ. We need God's Spirit to apply God's Word to our hearts so that we demonstrate both courage and compassion as we engage this issue.

---

[1] "Worldwide Abortion Statistics," *Abort73.com*, last modified May 26, 2011, http://www.abort73.com /abortion_facts/worldwide_abortion_statistics.

HOW GOD SEES
THE UNBORN

THE UNBORN MAY SEEM insignificant to many in our culture, but God cares deeply for them. Children in the womb are created in God's image and he knows them. We must therefore see and value the unborn as God does.

You formed my inward parts; you knitted me
together in my mother's womb. I praise you, for I
am fearfully and wonderfully made. Wonderful are
your works; my soul knows it very well. My frame
was not hidden from you, when I was being made in
secret, intricately woven in the depths of the earth.
Your eyes saw my unformed substance; in your book
were written, every one of them, the days that were
formed for me, when as yet there was none of them.

PSALM 139:13-16

You are he who took me from the womb; you made me trust you at my mother's breasts. On you was I cast from my birth, and from my mother's womb you have been my God.

PSALM 22:9-10

When Elizabeth heard the greeting of Mary, the baby leaped in her womb.

LUKE 1:41

Responding in Prayer

- Thank God for his miraculous work in creating and sustaining life. Acknowledge that he is the rightful owner of all people and things.
- Pray that God would help you see the unborn the way he sees them: as individuals made in his image.
- Ask God to cleanse you from any unconfessed sin of abortion, of encouraging others to have an abortion, or of standing by in silence. Receive his gift of forgiveness.

HOW WE SHOULD
RESPOND TO ABORTION

GOD'S PEOPLE MUST seek to defend those who cannot defend themselves. This kind of response will involve courageously speaking on behalf of the unborn, reaching out in love to mothers considering abortions, and making known the evil of abortion in our different areas of influence. Our conviction, however, must be marked by humility, for we know that those who disagree with us on this issue are also created in God's image. In the end, only God can bring about lasting change with regard to this evil, so we should plead with him in prayer.

> If you faint in the day of adversity, your strength is small. Rescue those who are being taken away to death; hold back those who are stumbling to the slaughter. If you say, "Behold, we did not know this," does not he who weighs the heart perceive it?

PROVERBS 24:10-12

Give justice to the weak and the fatherless; maintain the right of the afflicted and the destitute. Rescue the weak and the needy; deliver them from the hand of the wicked.

PSALM 82:3-4

Take no part in the unfruitful works of darkness, but instead expose them.

EPHESIANS 5:11

Responding in Prayer

- Ask God to give you faith and courage to speak up and act on behalf of the unborn.
- Pray that God would intervene and bring justice for the unborn. Ask that pro-abortion policies would be defeated and that leaders and politicians in favor of abortion would change their minds on this issue.
- Pray that God would use you and your church to minister to moms who are considering having an abortion.

ORPHANS
AND
WIDOWS

Religion that is pure and undefiled before

God the Father is this: to visit orphans

and widows in their affliction, and to keep

oneself unstained from the world.

JAMES 1:27

APPROXIMATELY 153 MILLION children around the world live as orphans, meaning that they have lost at least one parent. Included in that number are about eighteen million children who have lost both parents. Not included in that number, though, are the millions of effectively orphaned children who live in institutions or on the streets, in addition to vast multitudes who live as "social orphans," meaning that even if a parent is alive, the children rarely, if ever, see that parent or experience life as part of a family.[1]

When you add to the world's orphan crisis the 245 million widows—115 million of whom live in poverty and suffer from social isolation and economic deprivation as a result of losing their husbands—the problem can feel overwhelming.[2] However, Scripture teaches us that God knows and cares about the plight of orphans and widows. In fact, he tells his people throughout Scripture to take care of those in need. We are to imitate Jesus in reaching out to the destitute. And, as we provide for the physical needs of orphans and widows, we also point people to the one who provides ultimate security and protection through the gospel.

[1] "On Understanding Orphan Statistics," *Christian Alliance for Orphans*, accessed October 28, 2016, http://cafo.org/resource/on-understanding-orphan-statistics.
[2] Associated Press, "Report: Over 115 Million Widows Worldwide Live in Poverty," *USA Today*, June 23, 2010, http://usatoday30.usatoday.com/news/health/2010-06-23-un-widows-poverty_N.htm?csp=34news.

GOD'S CONCERN FOR ORPHANS AND WIDOWS

ALTHOUGH ORPHANS AND WIDOWS are often exploited or ignored by the world, God cares for them. They are created in his image and for his glory; therefore, the church ought to treat orphans and widows with justice and compassion. God warns us not to oppress the weak and needy. He is a God of justice.

You shall not mistreat any widow or fatherless child.

EXODUS 22:22

The LORD your God is God of gods and Lord of lords, the great, the mighty, and the awesome God, who is not partial and takes no bribe. He executes justice for the fatherless and the widow, and loves the sojourner, giving him food and clothing. Love the sojourner, therefore, for you were sojourners in the land of Egypt.

DEUTERONOMY 10:17-19

The LORD watches over the sojourners; he upholds the widow and the fatherless, but the way of the wicked he brings to ruin.

PSALM 146:9

Responding in Prayer

- Praise God for his compassion toward orphans and widows. Thank him for his kindness, mercy, and protection.
- Pray that God would open your eyes to opportunities to minister to widows and orphans in your own community.
- Thank God that he sees and punishes the injustice of those who oppress widows and orphans.

OUR RESPONSIBILITY TO ORPHANS AND WIDOWS

GOD COMMANDS HIS PEOPLE throughout Scripture to take care of those who have no family. The gospel of God's grace compels us to treat them fairly and to provide for them generously. We ought to speak out when orphans and widows are oppressed.

Learn to do good; seek justice, correct oppression; bring justice to the fatherless, plead the widow's cause.

ISAIAH 1:17

Religion that is pure and undefiled before God the Father is this: to visit orphans and widows in their affliction, and to keep oneself unstained from the world.

JAMES 1:27

Thus says the LORD: Do justice and righteousness,
and deliver from the hand of the oppressor him who
has been robbed. And do no wrong or violence to
the resident alien, the fatherless, and the widow, nor
shed innocent blood in this place.

JEREMIAH 22:3

Responding in Prayer

- Ask God what role he might have for you in terms of caring for orphans in your community.
- Pray for the widows in your church. Ask them how you can best serve them.
- Pray that God would give you the courage to speak up on behalf of those who are oppressed. Pray also that our political leaders would act with justice and mercy in relation to widows and orphans.

CONVICTION

If you faint in the day of adversity,

your strength is small.

PROVERBS 24:10

WE MUST NOT be intimidated by our culture's increasing hostility toward the gospel. In fact, Scripture teaches us to expect such opposition. As followers of Christ, we must speak against sin, injustice, and oppression, and we must hold to the truths of God's Word regardless of the cost. Christ's love should also compel us to share the gospel with the multiplied millions who have never even heard of God's salvation in Jesus Christ.

Thankfully, in his grace, God has not left us to engage culture in our own power and wisdom. He has given us his Spirit and his Word to help us stand. We can trust the God who has promised that his truth will prevail.

STANDING FOR THE TRUTH

GOD REPEATEDLY CALLS us to stand for the truth, even when the truth is unpopular. To maintain such conviction, we must be immersed in God's Word. No matter how our culture's views shift, God's people must seek to glorify him and to remain anchored in his truth.

> In the world you will have tribulation. But take heart; I [Jesus] have overcome the world.
>
> JOHN 16:33

> Fear not, for I am with you; be not dismayed, for I am your God; I will strengthen you, I will help you, I will uphold you with my righteous right hand.
>
> ISAIAH 41:10

> Peter and John answered them, "Whether it is right in the sight of God to listen to you rather than to

God, you must judge, for we cannot but speak of
what we have seen and heard."

ACTS 4:19-20

Responding in Prayer

- Ask God to give you a deeper love for him and for his
  Word. Pray that your desires would align with his will.
- Ask God to give you the strength to speak his truth
  into difficult situations.
- Pray that your church would remain faithful to the
  gospel and to all aspects of God's Word, regardless
  of the pressure of the surrounding culture.

SEX SLAVERY

Rescue the weak and the needy;

deliver them from the hand

of the wicked.

PSALM 82:4

APPROXIMATELY TWENTY-SEVEN MILLION people live in slavery today—more than at any other time in history.[1] That's millions of individuals made in the image of God who are being bought, sold, and exploited for sex in what has become one of the fastest-growing industries on earth.[2] And sex slavery isn't just a problem over *there*, far across the world; it's happening in our own communities and neighborhoods. God's people cannot remain ignorant of or apathetic to such evil.

We must confront the evil of sex slavery even as we show compassion toward its victims. God's concern for the weak and needy must be reflected in the church. Sadly, many Christians are actually contributing to the problem by using pornography, which fuels demand for more pornography, for research continually demonstrates a clear link between sex trafficking and the production of pornography. Rather than creating a demand for pornography and thus sex slavery, followers of Christ ought to be speaking out on behalf of the enslaved. As we act, we must trust in the Judge who will one day bring every sin, including sex slavery, to account.

[1] *End It*, http://enditmovement.com/about/#about; "The Problem," *The A21 Campaign*, http://www.a21 .org/content/human-trafficking/gloryw.

[2] "Trafficking and Slavery Fact Sheet," *Free the Slaves*, https://www.freetheslaves.net/wp-content/uploads /2016/03/FTS_factsheet-Updated2016.pdf; "Human Trafficking," *Polaris Project*, http://www.polarisproject .org/human-trafficking/overview.

GOD'S CONCERN FOR SEX SLAVES

GOD KNOWS AND CARES about everything that is done to those who are trafficked for sex. Even when no one else is paying attention, God sees their plight. On the other hand, if those who enslave others do not repent, they will face God's perfect justice on the last day.

Whoever steals a man and sells him, and anyone found in possession of him, shall be put to death.

EXODUS 21:16

[God] has pity on the weak and the needy, and saves the lives of the needy. From oppression and violence he redeems their life, and precious is their blood in his sight.

PSALM 72:13-14

[God] will judge the world in righteousness, and the peoples in his faithfulness.

PSALM 96:13

Responding in Prayer

- Thank God that he is just and that those who enslave others will be punished one day for their sin.
- Pray that God would mercifully spare many individuals who are now enslaved. Thank him for his compassion.
- Ask God to change the hearts of those who enslave others. Pray that these individuals would be transformed by the gospel.

OUR RESPONSE TO SEX SLAVERY

FOLLOWERS OF CHRIST must speak up and act on behalf of those who are oppressed through sex trafficking. Scripture calls us to expose evil and to help those in need. For some, this will mean being directly involved in the rescue of slaves. For others, involvement will take the form of giving to organizations that assist victims of sex slavery. All Christians, however, can pray for the safety and rescue of those who are enslaved.

> The earth is the LORD's, and everything in it, the world, and all who live in it; for he founded it upon the seas and established it upon the waters.
>
> PSALM 24:1-2, NIV

> When justice is done, it is a joy to the righteous but terror to evildoers.
>
> PROVERBS 21:15

The Spirit of the Sovereign LORD is on me,
because the LORD has anointed me to preach good
news to the poor. He has sent me to bind up the
brokenhearted, to proclaim freedom for the captives
and release from darkness for the prisoners, to
proclaim the year of the LORD's favor and the day of
vengeance of our God, to comfort all who mourn.

ISAIAH 61:1-2, NIV

Responding in Prayer

- Ask God to give you courage to speak up on behalf of
  the oppressed.
- Pray for ways that you or your church can be involved
  in ministering to those affected by human trafficking.
- Pray that God will help you trust his sovereignty,
  wisdom, and power in dealing with this evil.

MARRIAGE

A man shall leave his father and

his mother and hold fast to his wife,

and they shall become one flesh.

GENESIS 2:24

GOD HAS DESIGNED marriage to be a lifelong, monogamous relationship between a man and a woman. So intimate is this relationship that God calls it a one-flesh union. Our culture's attempt to redefine marriage, as well as its casual approach to divorce, is an assault on God's good design. Sadly, many professing Christians have bought into the culture's view of marriage.

The marriage of a man and a woman ultimately points to the relationship between Christ and his church. Christ has taken the church as his bride by dying for her. In response, the church is to be committed to Christ in faith and loving obedience. This covenant love will culminate in the age to come as we join Christ at the marriage supper of the Lamb (see Revelation 19:7).

GOD'S DESIGN FOR MARRIAGE

GOD CREATED THE INSTITUTION of marriage for our good and for his glory. When we, as followers of Christ, conform to God's design for marriage, we bear witness to Christ's love for the church. The church, as the bride of Christ, should look with eager expectation to the day when she will enjoy fellowship forever with her heavenly bridegroom.

A man shall leave his father and his mother and hold fast to his wife, and they shall become one flesh.

GENESIS 2:24

This mystery [concerning God's design for marriage] is profound, and I am saying that it refers to Christ and the church.

EPHESIANS 5:32

Let us rejoice and exult and give him the glory, for
the marriage of the Lamb has come, and his Bride
has made herself ready; it was granted her to clothe
herself with fine linen, bright and pure.

REVELATION 19:7-8

Responding in Prayer

- Thank God for his good design for marriage. Ask him
  to help you trust his design regardless of the opinions
  of others.
- Pray that God would strengthen the marriages in your
  church, including your own (if you are married), so
  that the proclamation of the gospel might be adorned
  by lives of faithfulness.
- Ask God to give you a greater love for Christ and a
  greater desire for his return.

LIVING FAITHFULLY
IN OUR MARRIAGES

MEN WHO LEAD their wives lovingly and sacrificially
bear witness to a Savior who gave his life for the church.
Likewise, wives bear witness to the truth when they respect
their husbands and gladly submit to their leadership. By
God's grace and with the help of his Spirit, followers of
Christ ought to be known for their faithfulness and selfless-
ness in marriage.

> An excellent wife who can find? She is far more
> precious than jewels. The heart of her husband trusts
> in her, and he will have no lack of gain. She does
> him good, and not harm, all the days of her life.
>
> PROVERBS 31:10-12

Wives, submit to your own husbands, as to the
Lord. For the husband is the head of the wife even
as Christ is the head of the church, his body, and
is himself its Savior. Now as the church submits to

Christ, so also wives should submit in everything to
their husbands.

Husbands, love your wives, as Christ loved the
church and gave himself up for her.

EPHESIANS 5:22-25

Wives, be subject to your own husbands, so that
even if some do not obey the word, they may be won
without a word by the conduct of their wives, when
they see your respectful and pure conduct. . . .

Likewise, husbands, live with your wives in an
understanding way, showing honor to the woman
as the weaker vessel, since they are heirs with you
of the grace of life, so that your prayers may not
be hindered.

1 PETER 3:1-2, 7

Responding in Prayer

- If you are married, ask God to strengthen your
  marriage and to show you areas where you need
  to grow. If you are single, ask God to expand your
  opportunities to serve him faithfully and effectively.
- Husbands, pray that God would give you courage to
  lead and a heart that is willing to sacrifice for your
  wife. Wives, pray that God would give you humility
  as you seek the good of your husband and submit to
  his leadership.
- Ask God to guard you from temptation and
  unfaithfulness in your marriage. Pray that he might
  give you a godly accountability partner.

SEXUAL MORALITY

The body is not meant for sexual immorality, but for the Lord.

1 CORINTHIANS 6:13

THE MARRIAGE OF a man and a woman is the only context in which God has designed the good gift of sex to be enjoyed, and God has set this boundary for our good. Many in our culture want to make their own decisions about what is sexually permissible, but Scripture tells us that our bodies belong to God. We must trust his wisdom and take seriously his warning that those who persist in sexual immorality will not inherit the Kingdom of God.

While it's easy to point the finger at our culture, we as Christians need to make sure that we are practicing what we preach. In addition to the sins that make the headlines (like homosexuality), sexual immorality shows up in a variety of other ways. If we are unfaithful in our marriages, if we are entertained by sexually explicit material, or if our thoughts are impure, then we too are sinning by going against God's good design. We must regularly seek God's help, as well as accountability from other Christians, as we aim to please God with our bodies and model for the world what it means to be devoted to the Lord.

WARNINGS AGAINST SEXUAL IMMORALITY

SATAN TEMPTS US with promises of sexual pleasure and fulfillment, but any sexual activity that is outside of God's design is eternally dangerous. God warns that those who refuse to repent of sexual immorality in various forms—whether it's homosexuality, adultery, etc.—will be barred from entering his Kingdom. Such warnings should compel us to flee sin and to pursue Christ, trusting fully in God's good design.

Do you not know that the unrighteous will not inherit the kingdom of God? Do not be deceived: neither the sexually immoral, nor idolaters, nor adulterers, nor men who practice homosexuality, nor thieves, nor the greedy, nor drunkards, nor revilers, nor swindlers will inherit the kingdom of God. And such were some of you. But you were washed, you were sanctified, you were justified in the name of the Lord Jesus Christ and by the Spirit of our God.

1 CORINTHIANS 6:9-11

You have heard that it was said, "You shall not commit adultery." But I say to you that everyone who looks at a woman with lustful intent has already committed adultery with her in his heart. If your right eye causes you to sin, tear it out and throw it away. For it is better that you lose one of your members than that your whole body be thrown into hell. And if your right hand causes you to sin, cut it off and throw it away. For it is better that you lose one of your members than that your whole body go into hell.

MATTHEW 5:27-30

This is the will of God, your sanctification: that you abstain from sexual immorality; that each one of you know how to control his own body in holiness and honor, not in the passion of lust like the Gentiles who do not know God; that no one transgress and wrong his brother in this matter, because the Lord is an avenger in all these things, as we told you beforehand and solemnly warned you. For God has not called us for impurity, but in holiness. Therefore whoever disregards this, disregards not man but God, who gives his Holy Spirit to you.

1 THESSALONIANS 4:3-8

Responding in Prayer

- Thank God for his kindness in warning us against sexual sin and for giving us his Spirit to help us flee from it.
- Ask God to guard your thoughts, words, and actions from sexual immorality. Find another trusted Christian to meet with for accountability.
- Pray that God would give your family and your church a good testimony in your community as you seek to grow in Christlikeness.

SEEKING GOD'S GRACE IN RESPONSE TO SEXUAL SIN

No SIN IS TOO GREAT for God's forgiveness, and that includes sexual sins. Anyone who repents of his or her sin and trusts in Christ—his perfect life, his substitutionary death, and his resurrection—receives the forgiveness of sins and eternal life. Once we become children of God, we are no longer slaves to sin, for the Spirit frees us to walk in obedience (even if it is imperfect in this life). We can, by the grace of God, glorify God with our bodies.

> If we confess our sins, he is faithful and just to forgive us our sins and to cleanse us from all unrighteousness. . . .
> My little children, I am writing these things to you so that you may not sin. But if anyone does sin, we have an advocate with the Father, Jesus Christ the righteous. He is the propitiation for our sins, and not for ours only but also for the sins of the whole world.
> I JOHN I:9; 2:I-2

Keep your heart with all vigilance, for from it flow
the springs of life.

PROVERBS 4:23

Let not sin therefore reign in your mortal body, to
make you obey its passions. Do not present your
members to sin as instruments for unrighteousness,
but present yourselves to God as those who have
been brought from death to life, and your members
to God as instruments for righteousness. For sin will
have no dominion over you, since you are not under
law but under grace.

ROMANS 6:12-14

Responding in Prayer

- Confess your sexual sins to God, and ask him for
  forgiveness. Pray for his strength to enable you to turn
  from these sins and walk in obedience.
- Thank God for his grace and mercy toward you.
  Praise Christ that his sacrifice was sufficient to atone
  for all your sins.
- Ask God to help you look to Christ for your
  righteousness and satisfaction.

COMPASSION

When [Jesus] went ashore he saw a

great crowd, and he had compassion

on them, because they were like

sheep without a shepherd.

MARK 6:34

AS WE STAND against injustice, it's easy to become angry with those who perpetrate evil. When it comes to those who practice and promote sexual immorality, for example, our reaction is sometimes one of disgust. While we *should* feel a sense of anger as we see the destructive effects of sin, we cannot forget that those caught in sin are the very people we're trying to reach with the gospel.

Were it not for God's grace, we too would be caught in any number of sins. God did not save us because we were more wise or obedient than others; he saved us out of sheer mercy. How then can we refuse to extend that mercy to others? And in light of the undeserved physical blessings we have received—food, family, shelter, protection, etc.—how can we not give generously to those in need? God blesses his people so that they will be a blessing. Compassion and generosity toward our neighbors are fruits of the gospel.

A COMPASSIONATE SAVIOR

WHEN WE THINK about compassion, there is no better model than the Lord Jesus himself. As the Son of God, he would have been perfectly just to punish those who rejected him, and yet he responded with compassion. Jesus commands us to do the same. We need regular reminders that God has shown compassion to us so that we might show it to others.

> The Pharisees and their scribes grumbled at his disciples, saying, "Why do you eat and drink with tax collectors and sinners?" And Jesus answered them, "Those who are well have no need of a physician, but those who are sick. I have not come to call the righteous but sinners to repentance."
>
> LUKE 5:30-32

You have heard that it was said, "You shall love your neighbor and hate your enemy." But I say to you, Love your enemies and pray for those who persecute you, so that you may be sons of your Father who is in heaven. For he makes his sun rise on the evil and on the good, and sends rain on the just and on the unjust. For if you love those who love you, what reward do you have? Do not even the tax collectors do the same? And if you greet only your brothers, what more are you doing than others? Do not even the Gentiles do the same? You therefore must be perfect, as your heavenly Father is perfect.

MATTHEW 5:43-48

Remind them to be submissive to rulers and authorities, to be obedient, to be ready for every good work, to speak evil of no one, to avoid quarreling, to be gentle, and to show perfect courtesy toward all people. For we ourselves were once foolish, disobedient, led astray, slaves to various passions and pleasures, passing our days in malice and envy, hated by others and hating one another. But when the goodness and loving kindness of God our Savior appeared, he saved us, not because of works done by us in righteousness, but according to his own mercy, by the washing of regeneration and renewal of the Holy Spirit, whom he poured out on us richly through Jesus Christ our Savior, so that being justified by his grace we might become heirs according to the hope of eternal life.

TITUS 3:1-7

Responding in Prayer

- Thank God for his compassion toward you in Jesus Christ. Praise him for his mercy.
- Ask God to give you compassion for those who disagree with or oppose you.
- Pray that your church would be known for mercy and compassion toward sinners.

ETHNICITY

God created man in his own image.

GENESIS 1:27

ALTHOUGH OUR CULTURE has made some strides in treating people of all ethnicities and backgrounds with justice and mercy, we have a long way to go. Sadly, the same holds true for many churches. We must remember that our neighbor's value is not based on his or her skin color, economic status, or ethnic background, but rather on the fact that all people are created in God's image.

We should repent of any sense of superiority we feel toward others. God has commanded us to love our neighbors, regardless of our differences. The love of Christ ought to compel us to spread his gospel to people of all ethnicities and to partner with believers of all ethnicities. A multiethnic church is truly a countercultural witness in our culture.

HOW GOD SEES PEOPLE OF DIFFERENT ETHNICITIES

THE WORLD OFTEN assigns value based on what people look like, where they live, how much money they make, etc. Scripture, on the other hand, teaches that our value and dignity is based on the fact that God has created us in his image and for his glory. God desires for people of all ethnicities to be saved.

God created man in his own image, in the image of God he created him; male and female he created them.

GENESIS 1:27

[God] made from one man every nation of mankind to live on all the face of the earth, having determined allotted periods and the boundaries of their dwelling place.

ACTS 17:26

After this I looked, and behold, a great multitude
that no one could number, from every nation, from
all tribes and peoples and languages, standing before
the throne and before the Lamb, clothed in white
robes, with palm branches in their hands, and crying
out with a loud voice, "Salvation belongs to our God
who sits on the throne, and to the Lamb!"

REVELATION 7:9-10

Responding in Prayer

- Thank God that he is the Creator of all peoples and
  that he cares for them.
- Ask God to help you value people based on their
  relationship to him and not based on worldly
  standards.
- Pray that leaders in your own community and in
  our country would treat all ethnicities justly and
  mercifully.

HOW WE SHOULD TREAT PEOPLE OF DIFFERENT ETHNICITIES

THE COMMAND TO LOVE our neighbor means that we are to treat all people with respect, love, and compassion. We must speak up on their behalf, take care of their needs, and, most important, share the gospel with them. Scripture portrays Christ's bride (the church) as multiethnic, which means that our mission should extend to all peoples, languages, tribes, and tongues.

You shall love your neighbor as yourself.

MATTHEW 22:39

Go therefore and make disciples of all nations.

MATTHEW 28:19

[Peter] said to them, "You yourselves know how unlawful it is for a Jew to associate with or to visit anyone of another nation, but God has shown

me that I should not call any person common or
unclean."
ACTS 10:28

Responding in Prayer

- Ask God to give you courage to speak up on behalf
  of those who are ignored or oppressed in your own
  community and around the world.
- Pray that God would open doors for you to share the
  gospel with friends and neighbors who are different
  from you socially, economically, and ethnically.
- Ask God to help your church reach out to individuals
  of different ethnicities and to partner with gospel-
  believing churches that look different from yours.

THE REFUGEE CRISIS

You shall not wrong a sojourner

or oppress him, for you were

sojourners in the land of Egypt.

EXODUS 22:21

THROUGHOUT THE WORLD, the number of people displaced, put in danger, or forced from their homes right now is historically unprecedented. In Syria alone, half of the population—that's eleven million people—has either been displaced or killed.[1] Many people are divided over what to do with these individuals, and the issue is undoubtedly complex. Nevertheless, as followers of Christ, we have an obligation to minister to refugees, for they are made in God's image and many are in desperate need of the gospel.

Rather than seeing refugees as a political problem, Christians around the world ought to be eager to address their urgent physical and spiritual needs. Many of these people have never even heard the gospel, which means that we have an opportunity to reach the unreached right in our own backyards. Our response should not be driven by fear, but rather by faith. We should remember that it is only by God's grace that we are not refugees. How, then, can we fail to extend to others the compassion that Christ has shown to us?

[1] Ian Black, "Report on Syria Conflict Finds 11.5% of Population Killed or Injured," *The Guardian*, February 10, 2016, https://www.theguardian.com/world/2016/feb/11/report-on-syria-conflict-finds-115-of-population-killed-or-injured.

HOW GOD SEES REFUGEES

THE GOD WHO CARES for the afflicted, the weak, and the needy also cares for refugees. They too are created in his image and for his glory. God reminds his people in the Old Testament that they were sojourners in Egypt before he redeemed them. Today God's people are called sojourners (see 1 Peter 2:11) because we are looking to our promised reward—a better, heavenly country (see Hebrews 11:13-16).

> The LORD watches over the sojourners; he upholds the widow and the fatherless, but the way of the wicked he brings to ruin.
>
> PSALM 146:9

> Do not rob the poor, because he is poor, or crush the afflicted at the gate, for the LORD will plead their cause and rob of life those who rob them.
>
> PROVERBS 22:22-23

He [Jesus] came and preached peace to you who
were far off and peace to those who were near. For
through him we both have access in one Spirit to
the Father. So then you are no longer strangers and
aliens, but you are fellow citizens with the saints
and members of the household of God, built on the
foundation of the apostles and prophets, Christ Jesus
himself being the cornerstone, in whom the whole
structure, being joined together, grows into a holy
temple in the Lord.

EPHESIANS 2:17-21

Responding in Prayer

- Thank God for his kindness toward you in providing
  for your physical needs and for the ability to gather
  with other Christians. Pray that your gratitude would
  result in generosity and compassion toward others.
- Ask God to provide for the physical needs of refugees
  around the world. Pray for political leaders to treat
  refugees justly and with compassion.
- Pray that churches around the world would have
  opportunities to share the gospel with refugees.

OUR RESPONSIBILITY
TO REFUGEES

WHILE REFUGEES ARE OFTEN ignored or mistreated, Israel was told to be merciful toward sojourners. The same principle holds true today, as Christ told us to look at everyone as our neighbor. Christians should also reach out to refugees in obedience to the great commission. Christ sent us to make disciples of all nations, and that includes those who are forced from their homeland.

> You shall not oppress a sojourner. You know the heart of a sojourner, for you were sojourners in the land of Egypt.
>
> EXODUS 23:9

A lawyer stood up to put [Jesus] to the test, saying, "Teacher, what shall I do to inherit eternal life?" He said to him, "What is written in the Law? How do you read it?" And he answered, "You shall love the Lord

your God with all your heart and with all your soul
and with all your strength and with all your mind, and
your neighbor as yourself." And he said to him, "You
have answered correctly; do this, and you will live."

But he, desiring to justify himself, said to Jesus,
"And who is my neighbor?" Jesus replied, "A man
was going down from Jerusalem to Jericho, and he
fell among robbers, who stripped him and beat him
and departed, leaving him half dead. Now by chance
a priest was going down that road, and when he
saw him he passed by on the other side. So likewise
a Levite, when he came to the place and saw him,
passed by on the other side. But a Samaritan, as he
journeyed, came to where he was, and when he saw
him, he had compassion. He went to him and bound
up his wounds, pouring on oil and wine. Then he set
him on his own animal and brought him to an inn
and took care of him. And the next day he took out
two denarii and gave them to the innkeeper, saying,
'Take care of him, and whatever more you spend, I
will repay you when I come back.' Which of these
three, do you think, proved to be a neighbor to the
man who fell among the robbers?" He said, "The
one who showed him mercy." And Jesus said to him,
"You go, and do likewise."

LUKE 10:25-37

All authority in heaven and on earth has been given
to me [Jesus]. Go therefore and make disciples of all
nations, baptizing them in the name of the Father

and of the Son and of the Holy Spirit, teaching them to observe all that I have commanded you. And behold, I am with you always, to the end of the age.

MATTHEW 28:18-20

Responding in Prayer

- Pray that God would give you a generous heart toward refugees. Ask God to help you see them as people made in his image.
- Pray that the people of your community would treat refugees fairly and with compassion.
- Ask God to open doors for your church to minister to refugees and immigrants in your community.

RELIGIOUS LIBERTY

We must obey God rather than men.

ACTS 5:29

THE KIND OF FAITH that saves cannot be forced or coerced. A person must willingly believe in Christ and submit to his lordship in order to be a Christian. That's one of the reasons we should pray that our government, as well as governments around the world, will protect the free exercise of religion. Such freedom does not necessarily lead to agreement among religious groups, but it does respect some of the basic rights that should be afforded to all individuals. It also paves the way for the proclamation of the gospel.

It is tempting to get angry or to panic as it becomes more difficult to live out our faith. However, Scripture teaches that opposition to the gospel is to be expected. In fact, many of our brothers and sisters in Christ around the world face intense forms of persecution for their faith. We have much to learn from these believers as they continue to confess Christ in the face of social, economic, and physical persecution. We need to seek God's help so that we too will persevere until the end.

OUR OBLIGATION
TO GOVERNMENT

WE ARE OBLIGATED to submit to our government, for God
has instituted it for our good. God has also told us to pray
for our political leaders. As followers of Christ, we are
not to be known for disrespecting or disregarding those
in authority over us. However, when government commands us to do what God forbids, or when it forbids us
to do what God commands, we must choose to obey God,
regardless of the consequences.

Let every person be subject to the governing
authorities. For there is no authority except from
God, and those that exist have been instituted by
God. Therefore whoever resists the authorities resists
what God has appointed, and those who resist will
incur judgment. For rulers are not a terror to good
conduct, but to bad. Would you have no fear of the
one who is in authority? Then do what is good, and

you will receive his approval, for he is God's servant
for your good. But if you do wrong, be afraid, for he
does not bear the sword in vain. For he is the servant
of God, an avenger who carries out God's wrath on
the wrongdoer. Therefore one must be in subjection,
not only to avoid God's wrath but also for the sake
of conscience. For because of this you also pay taxes,
for the authorities are ministers of God, attending to
this very thing. Pay to all what is owed to them: taxes
to whom taxes are owed, revenue to whom revenue
is owed, respect to whom respect is owed, honor to
whom honor is owed.

ROMANS 13:1-7

First of all, then, I urge that supplications, prayers,
intercessions, and thanksgivings be made for all
people, for kings and all who are in high positions,
that we may lead a peaceful and quiet life, godly
and dignified in every way. This is good, and it is
pleasing in the sight of God our Savior, who desires
all people to be saved and to come to the knowledge
of the truth. For there is one God, and there is one
mediator between God and men, the man Christ
Jesus, who gave himself as a ransom for all, which
is the testimony given at the proper time.

I TIMOTHY 2:1-6

When they had brought [the apostles], they set them
before the council. And the high priest questioned
them, saying, "We strictly charged you not to teach

in this name, yet here you have filled Jerusalem with your teaching, and you intend to bring this man's blood upon us." But Peter and the apostles answered, "We must obey God rather than men."

ACTS 5:27-29

Responding in Prayer

- Thank God for instituting government for our good and for the freedoms our government upholds.
- Pray for your government leaders that they might rule justly and with compassion. Pray also that they might be saved.
- Ask God to give you wisdom and courage as you seek to discern when it is necessary to disobey the government.

RESPONDING
TO PERSECUTION

THOSE WHO FOLLOW Jesus should expect to suffer for their faith. In fact, God's Word says this kind of suffering is a blessing. This does not mean suffering is easy or to be sought after, but it does mean that we can have hope in the midst of it. We should also remember that we are members of a larger body of believers—both in terms of our local church and in terms of God's people spread across the globe. We should pray for, weep with, and speak up for our brothers and sisters in Christ who suffer. We should plead with God to protect them, to provide for their needs, and ultimately to sustain their faith to the end.

> To this you have been called, because Christ also
> suffered for you, leaving you an example, so that
> you might follow in his steps. He committed no sin,
> neither was deceit found in his mouth. When he was
> reviled, he did not revile in return; when he suffered,
> he did not threaten, but continued entrusting himself

to him who judges justly. He himself bore our sins
in his body on the tree, that we might die to sin and
live to righteousness. By his wounds you have been
healed. For you were straying like sheep, but have now
returned to the Shepherd and Overseer of your souls.

I PETER 2:21-25

Blessed are those who are persecuted for righteousness'
sake, for theirs is the kingdom of heaven.

Blessed are you when others revile you and
persecute you and utter all kinds of evil against you
falsely on my account. Rejoice and be glad, for your
reward is great in heaven, for so they persecuted the
prophets who were before you.

MATTHEW 5:10-12

Remember those who are in prison, as though in
prison with them, and those who are mistreated,
since you also are in the body.

HEBREWS 13:3

Responding in Prayer

- Pray that God would sustain your faith through trials
  that come on account of your witness.
- Pray for God to sustain the faith of persecuted
  believers around the world. Ask him to provide for
  their needs and to use their witness for the spread
  of the gospel.
- Ask God to thwart the persecution and unjust
  treatment of Christians around the world.

COURAGE

The LORD is my light and my salvation;

whom shall I fear?

The LORD is the stronghold of my life;

of whom shall I be afraid?

PSALM 27:1

IT SHOULD COME as no surprise to followers of a crucified Savior that speaking the truth is often costly. The world hates the light and those who bear witness to the light. Therefore, we need God's help as we speak to a culture that is increasingly opposed to our message.

God knows that we are weak and that we are prone to fear. To combat such fear, God has given us his Spirit as well as many hope-filled promises in Scripture. We can be assured that, as we engage culture, our God will be with us.

SEEKING GOD'S GRACE AND STRENGTH

GOD NOT ONLY tells us to speak truth in the face of opposition but he also empowers us to do it. One of the ways God moves us to act is by applying the promises of Scripture to our hearts by his Spirit. The God who has all power and authority will strengthen his people to do his will. The fearful can look to God for courage.

> When I am afraid, I put my trust in you.
>
> PSALM 56:3

Have no fear of them, for nothing is covered that will not be revealed, or hidden that will not be known. What I tell you in the dark, say in the light, and what you hear whispered, proclaim on the housetops. And do not fear those who kill the body but cannot kill the soul. Rather fear him who can destroy both soul and body in hell. Are not two

sparrows sold for a penny? And not one of them will
fall to the ground apart from your Father. But even
the hairs of your head are all numbered. Fear not,
therefore; you are of more value than many sparrows.
So everyone who acknowledges me before men, I
also will acknowledge before my Father who is in
heaven, but whoever denies me before men, I also
will deny before my Father who is in heaven.

MATTHEW 10:26-33

God is our refuge and strength, a very present help
in trouble. Therefore we will not fear though the
earth gives way, though the mountains be moved
into the heart of the sea, though its waters roar and
foam, though the mountains tremble at its swelling.

PSALM 46:1-3

Responding in Prayer

- Thank God that he is working all things together for
  your good (see Romans 8:28) and that he is always
  present with you.
- Confess to God your weakness and fear. Ask him to
  strengthen you and to remove the fear of other people.
- Pray for the courage to share the gospel and to speak
  out on difficult issues.

THE UNREACHED

How are they to believe in him

of whom they have never heard?

ROMANS 10:14

SADLY, THERE ARE still more than six thousand people groups classified as unreached. That's more than three billion people who have never even heard the gospel.[1] These are startling numbers, especially given what's at stake. Scripture teaches that everyone who dies without believing the gospel will face the just punishment for their sins: God's eternal judgment in hell.

When we consider the spiritual state of the unreached, as well as Christ's command to make disciples of all nations (see Matthew 28:18-20), we should be compelled to take this gospel to everyone. However, it's not guilt that compels us, for we have freely received God's undeserved salvation. Followers of Christ ought to be compelled by grace. Even so, we recognize that this mission is costly and that it will require sacrifice. In the end, though, we'll find that Christ's reward was worth everything we gave up.

---

[1] To be classified as unreached means that less than 2 percent of the total population confesses the gospel and believes the Bible. See *PeopleGroups*, accessed October 28, 2016, http://www.peoplegroups.org; *Joshua Project*, accessed October 28, 2016, http://www.joshuaproject.net.

THE SPIRITUAL STATE
OF THE UNREACHED

SCRIPTURE IS CLEAR that a person must hear and believe the gospel in order to be saved. This is why the early disciples, as well as Christians throughout church history, made great sacrifices to make Christ known. Apart from the gospel, we remain dead in our sins. We would do well to reflect on the desperate condition of those who have not heard about God's saving love in Jesus Christ.

> You were dead in the trespasses and sins in which you once walked, following the course of this world, following the prince of the power of the air, the spirit that is now at work in the sons of disobedience— among whom we all once lived in the passions of our flesh, carrying out the desires of the body and the mind, and were by nature children of wrath, like the rest of mankind.
>
> EPHESIANS 2:1-3

There is salvation in no one else, for there is no other name under heaven given among men by which we must be saved.

ACTS 4:12

There is no distinction between Jew and Greek; for the same Lord is Lord of all, bestowing his riches on all who call on him. For "everyone who calls on the name of the Lord will be saved."

How then will they call on him in whom they have not believed? And how are they to believe in him of whom they have never heard? And how are they to hear without someone preaching? And how are they to preach unless they are sent? As it is written, "How beautiful are the feet of those who preach the good news!" But they have not all obeyed the gospel. For Isaiah says, "Lord, who has believed what he has heard from us?" So faith comes from hearing, and hearing through the word of Christ.

ROMANS 10:12-17

Responding in Prayer

- Thank God for his grace in making the gospel known to you and for opening your heart to believe.
- Ask God to send gospel workers into the field of the unreached (see Matthew 9:37-38). Pray that many would hear and believe.
- Ask the Lord to open up opportunities for your church to partner with missionaries on the field that are seeking to reach the unreached.

THE COST AND REWARD OF GOING TO THE UNREACHED

Jesus repeatedly told his disciples that following him would cost them everything. They would have to die to themselves—forsaking their comfort, their dreams, and even their own safety. However, Jesus also told his disciples that the reward for following him would outweigh the cost. The New Testament speaks of this reward when it talks about realities like eternal life, our future inheritance, and a new creation. We take the gospel to difficult places and to dangerous people groups because we want these individuals to join with us in eternal fellowship with Jesus Christ.

As they were going along the road, someone said to him, "I will follow you wherever you go." And Jesus said to him, "Foxes have holes, and birds of the air have nests, but the Son of Man has nowhere to lay his head." To another he said, "Follow me." But he said, "Lord, let me first go and bury my father." And

Jesus said to him, "Leave the dead to bury their own dead. But as for you, go and proclaim the kingdom of God." Yet another said, "I will follow you, Lord, but let me first say farewell to those at my home." Jesus said to him, "No one who puts his hand to the plow and looks back is fit for the kingdom of God."

LUKE 9:57-62

The sufferings of this present time are not worth comparing with the glory that is to be revealed to us.

ROMANS 8:18

After this I looked, and behold, a great multitude that no one could number, from every nation, from all tribes and peoples and languages, standing before the throne and before the Lamb, clothed in white robes, with palm branches in their hands, and crying out with a loud voice, "Salvation belongs to our God who sits on the throne, and to the Lamb!"

REVELATION 7:9-10

Responding in Prayer

- Pray that God would work in you so that you would continue to grow in Christlikeness. Ask him to help you put to death sinful and selfish desires.
- Ask God to give you faith and joy as you consider the sufferings of this life in light of your eternal reward.
- Pray that your church would be generous in using its resources to get the gospel to the unreached.

THE CHURCH'S WITNESS

By this all people will know that you are my

disciples, if you have love for one another.

JOHN 13:35

GOD NEVER INTENDED for you to live the Christian life by yourself. The first Christians immediately started meeting together and lived under the apostles' teaching in close fellowship (see Acts 2:42-47). Of course, the world didn't always approve of the early church's message, but unbelievers were struck as they observed this unusual, close-knit community. No individual Christian could have this kind of gospel witness.

Jesus said that the world would be able to identify his disciples by their love for one another (see John 13:35). It's fitting, then, that Paul gave his churches so many instructions about how they were to love, forgive, and care for one another (see Romans 12:9-13; Ephesians 4:25-32). A culture that rejects Christ needs to both hear the gospel and also see a community of people transformed by the gospel. In addition to the church's collective witness, we (as individual Christians) need the prayer and support of other believers as we speak and act in ways that are strange or even offensive to the surrounding culture.

IT'S NOT UP TO YOU

WE OFTEN LOOK to those who are strong, wise, and influential to solve the world's problems, but God repeatedly reminds his people that he is their strength and that he will accomplish his purposes. Embracing this truth empowers us to persevere in hope, even as we address widespread injustice and sin. Living faithfully in a godless culture requires trusting in a sovereign and gracious God.

> You keep him in perfect peace whose mind is stayed on you, because he trusts in you.
> ISAIAH 26:3

Thus says the LORD: "Heaven is my throne, and the earth is my footstool; what is the house that you would build for me, and what is the place of my rest? All these things my hand has made, and so all these things came to be, declares the LORD. But this is

the one to whom I will look: he who is humble and
contrite in spirit and trembles at my word."

ISAIAH 66:1-2

The LORD looks down from heaven; he sees all the
children of man; from where he sits enthroned he
looks out on all the inhabitants of the earth, he who
fashions the hearts of them all and observes all their
deeds. The king is not saved by his great army; a
warrior is not delivered by his great strength. The
war horse is a false hope for salvation, and by its
great might it cannot rescue.

Behold, the eye of the LORD is on those who fear
him, on those who hope in his steadfast love, that
he may deliver their soul from death and keep them
alive in famine.

Our soul waits for the LORD; he is our help and
our shield. For our heart is glad in him, because
we trust in his holy name. Let your steadfast love,
O LORD, be upon us, even as we hope in you.

PSALM 33:13-22

Responding in Prayer

- Confess your anxieties to God, and ask him to forgive
  you for the times you haven't trusted him. Pray that
  he would strengthen your faith.
- Praise God for his sovereignty, wisdom, and power.
  Express your trust in him, and confess that you are
  not strong enough to overcome evil on your own.
- Ask God to use your efforts and abilities for his glory.

A GROUP EFFORT

THE NEW TESTAMENT knows nothing of individual Christians who are living for Jesus on their own. Every follower of Christ should be in fellowship with a local body of believers. Christ gave his life for the church, and it is the church that has been tasked with making disciples of all nations (see Matthew 28:18-20). Those who gather regularly for corporate worship spread out to share the gospel with others throughout the week.

> A new commandment I [Jesus] give to you, that you love one another: just as I have loved you, you also are to love one another. By this all people will know that you are my disciples, if you have love for one another.
>
> JOHN 13:34-35

Look carefully then how you walk, not as unwise but as wise, making the best use of the time, because the days are evil. Therefore do not be foolish, but understand what the will of the Lord is. And do not get drunk with wine, for that is debauchery, but be filled with the Spirit, addressing one another in psalms and hymns and spiritual songs, singing and making melody to the Lord with your heart, giving thanks always and for everything to God the Father in the name of our Lord Jesus Christ, submitting to one another out of reverence for Christ.

EPHESIANS 5:15-21

Husbands, love your wives, as Christ loved the church and gave himself up for her, that he might sanctify her, having cleansed her by the washing of water with the word, so that he might present the church to himself in splendor, without spot or wrinkle or any such thing, that she might be holy and without blemish.

EPHESIANS 5:25-27

Responding in Prayer

- Thank God for the gift of the church and the grace he supplies through the ministry of other believers.
- Pray that the members of your church would be known in your community for their sacrificial love for one another.
- Ask God to use your church to proclaim the gospel throughout your community. Pray that your church would adorn the gospel as it takes care of the needy and as it addresses sin and injustice.

FOUND FAITHFUL

GOD'S PLAN FOR YOU may not be to change the world, but he does want you to be faithful with the opportunities he has given you. It's also helpful to remember that God does not evaluate our efforts like the world does. The fruits of our labors may be hidden, or perhaps our message will be rejected. Still, we can rest assured that God sees and knows all things. And even when we fall short, which will be often, he has more than enough grace to cover our sins and shortcomings.

Trust in the LORD with all your heart, and do not lean on your own understanding. In all your ways acknowledge him, and he will make straight your paths.

PROVERBS 3:5-6

Consider your calling, brothers: not many of you were wise according to worldly standards, not many were powerful, not many were of noble birth. But

God chose what is foolish in the world to shame the
wise; God chose what is weak in the world to shame
the strong; God chose what is low and despised
in the world, even things that are not, to bring to
nothing things that are, so that no human being
might boast in the presence of God. And because
of him you are in Christ Jesus, who became to us
wisdom from God, righteousness and sanctification
and redemption, so that, as it is written, "Let the one
who boasts, boast in the Lord."

I CORINTHIANS 1:26-31

One who is faithful in a very little is also faithful in
much, and one who is dishonest in a very little is
also dishonest in much. If then you have not been
faithful in the unrighteous wealth, who will entrust
to you the true riches? And if you have not been
faithful in that which is another's, who will give
you that which is your own?

LUKE 16:10-12

Responding in Prayer

- Thank God for the grace he has shown you in the
  gospel.
- Pray that God would open your eyes to the needs
  around you and that he would use you to point others
  to Christ.
- Ask God to strengthen your faith so you can persevere
  through trials. Pray that you would fear God and rest
  in his sovereignty rather than fearing people.

CLOSING PRAYER

WHEN JESUS TAUGHT his disciples to pray, he told them to pray for God's Kingdom to come and for God's will to be done (see Matthew 6:10). That request should undergird everything we've prayed about over the past month. Whether it's poverty, abortion, marriage, refugees, or any other issue, we want God's purposes to be carried out. But we're not merely spectators: we're also praying that God would use us to accomplish his will.

As God's people, we can have complete confidence knowing that evil and sin will not go unpunished and that God's promised redemption will be consummated at Christ's coming. While we wait for that day, we must stand fast in the hope of the gospel and be faithful where God has placed us. And we cannot forget that our service to Christ is itself a gift of God's grace. We work in the power of his Spirit and for his glory.

I am not ashamed of the gospel, for it is the power of God for salvation to everyone who believes, to the Jew first and also to the Greek.

ROMANS 1:16

Now may the God of peace himself sanctify you completely, and may your whole spirit and soul and body be kept blameless at the coming of our Lord Jesus Christ. He who calls you is faithful; he will surely do it.

1 THESSALONIANS 5:23-24

Then I saw a new heaven and a new earth, for the first heaven and the first earth had passed away, and the sea was no more. And I saw the holy city, new Jerusalem, coming down out of heaven from God, prepared as a bride adorned for her husband. And I heard a loud voice from the throne saying, "Behold, the dwelling place of God is with man. He will dwell with them, and they will be his people, and God himself will be with them as their God. He will wipe away every tear from their eyes, and death shall be no more, neither shall there be mourning, nor crying, nor pain anymore, for the former things have passed away."

REVELATION 21:1-4

Responding in Prayer

- Ask God to give you a greater desire for his glory and for his will to be carried out on earth as it is in heaven.

- Ask God to strengthen you by his Spirit so that you might walk faithfully where he has placed you. Pray for humility, boldness, and a love for others.
- Pray that God would direct you and your church to specific needs in your community and among the nations. Ask him to help you address these needs by trusting in the power of the gospel.